HANG-UPS

poems

C. J. Stevens

Published by John Wade, Publisher
Box 303, Phillips, Maine 04966

HANG-UPS
Library of Congress Catalog No. 93-60823
  ISBN # 1-882425-00-6 (cloth)
  ISBN # 1-882425-01-4 (paperback)

First Edition
Printed in the United States of America

ACKNOWLEDGMENTS

I thank the editors of the following publications in which many of these poems first appeared: *American Weave, Ann Arbor Review, Ante, Aspect Magazine, The Cathartic, El Corno Emplumado, Empire, Free Lance, The Galley Sail Review, Hollow Spring Review, Mountain Summer, New Frontiers* (England), *Nightshade, Ore* (England), *The Panhandler, Peace and Freedom* (England), *Poetry Forum, Poetry Now, The Post Crescent, Red Cedar Review, Road Apple Review, Screen Door Review, The Smith,* and *Wormwood Review.*

Further acknowledgments are made to the publishers of these anthologies: *Aspect Anthology; Beat, Street & Easy: The Other American Anthology;* and *Stoogism Anthology.*

Several of these poems have appeared in collections with the following presses: *The Crossing Press, Icarus Press, Juniper Press, Poet & Printer* (England), and *Sparrow Press.*

The Dutch and Flemish translations have been published in the following magazines: *Cape Rock Quarterly, Cardinal, College Arts, Connecticut Fireside, Corduroy, El Corno Emplumado, Gamut Magazine, Hika, The Old Red Kimono, Poet Lore, Poetry Dial, The Promethean Lamp, Resurgence* (England), *Sou'wester, Trace,* and *Webster Review.*

Several of the translations have been printed in these anthologies: "Dutch Interiors," *Columbia University Press;* and "Carpet of Sparrows," (title of the book taken from "In the Park" translation) *Nocturnal Canary Press.*

I thank the publishers who have printed these translations in collections: "Poems from the Lowlands," *A Small Pond Book;* "Waterland: A Gathering from Holland," *Holmgangers Press;* and "From the Flemish of Gaston Burssens," *Arts End Books.*

CONTENTS

I HANG-UPS

ELEGY FOR A BASTARD BROTHER

Somewhere in the mix-up of flesh and blood
you were born full grown when I was twenty-one.
I didn't think of you as someone living—
you were an apparition in our skeletal closet.
But I began to find traces of your presence
in the flinty pupils of my mother's eyes
as she stirred her cauldron of memories
and spoke of our father's excesses and lies.
Finally, you became a witness of unfaithfulness,
though my mother insisted that you were blameless.
One night you spoke to me in a dream,
and the door of the closet was open like a womb.
I never mentioned your name, never said James,
but I would sometimes imagine your face
haunting my face as I searched for resemblances
in the bold world of a mirror. Adulthood,
marriage, the birth of my son—these kept you hidden.
Before our father died I wanted to tell you
how tolerance sweetened his well-lived face.
I don't know why I never tried to find you;
why I waited until it was too late.
The news of your death left me featureless.
You weren't even old—just someone called James.

THE RAGGED WORLD OF ELDERS

I first began to see my elders piece by piece;
began to measure them by coats and hats.
I saw how the day seemed tattered as they walked
and how they fell away in rags. And once
I saw sharkskin thrown over gingham
in a room the moon had stitched white—my elders.
Piece by piece I began to measure; I watched
the scene over and over; I wanted to see
the whole cloth. I didn't know why
all was unraveling in the ragged world of elders.

AT THE CORN'S EDGE

After an afternoon of hide-and-seek behind the shed
three of us went out where the cornstalks were.
There wasn't much to hear: there were the gossipy
leaves of corn and something rubbing against the stalks
twenty rows over. Ten rows from the racket
we stopped. Someone was dying we thought;
someone was crying, maybe moaning, and it didn't
sound right in the corn. We crept closer.
Five rows from the killing we stopped. We didn't think
dying should take so long. We were shocked,
of course! Who wouldn't be when seeing what we saw?
A man and woman were wrestling at the edge of the field,
wrestling for all they worth, right there
on the cold ground with only the drooping corn
to keep the wind from stinging their bare asses.
Why they should want to fight with nothing on
or injure themselves on the thinned-out corn stubbles,
we couldn't say. It didn't seem right to stop them
and ask. We didn't know the fellow, but the woman
on the ground was my second cousin Ann. She made
all the noise. He just grunted and the yellow
cornstalks shook and the stubbles crackled; then they began
to wrestle all over. Who would think a girl as frail
as cousin Ann would wrestle that buck of a stranger
at the corn's edge a mile from town? To hear her wail
and carry on, one could tell she loved to fight. His hair
she pulled, but he was on top, and the three of us thought
he won. Ann wasn't a girl to keep a grudge longer
than she had to. Later, when they put their clothes on,
she smiled. Ann's a nice kid. But the stranger was stronger.

OLD SONG

How in the hell
kin the old folks tell
it ain't gonna
rain no more?

My father would sing
it through and tap
one shoe upon
the floor and sway
before the mirror.

Then puritanical
grandfather would look
at my mother and say:
"The damned fool!"

And laugh.

GREAT-GRANDMOTHER CATHARINE

Grandfather always said
his mother was a no-
nonsense woman; never known
to be frivolous, maddeningly
exact, and puritanical.

Father called her a bitch.
Her appetite for scandal
was insatiable; her slyness
was immense. He said
she led her eight bedeviled children
a witches' dance.

         Aunt Helen
compared her to New England
granite. Helen thought a mountain
of rock had to be hauled
from the wilderness when God
decided to raise Catharine's
fortress of perseverance
and courage.

         Cousin Ed
remembered her kindness;
Uncle Mearl saved her poems
for me to save; her few
surviving neighbors spoke
longingly of her cheeses and cakes;
Cousin Ethemer gave me

her photograph to keep.

                   I once
had that portrait hanging in
a conspicuous place. Daily,
I saw the quarried hatred
in those disapproving eyes.
I tried to imagine kindness
warming that bygone face.

And that New England storm,
still trapped behind her brow,
puzzles me—even now.
I think of her pinched mouth,
longing, no doubt, to open wide,
to scold or hurt me somehow.

PURITAN BEGINNINGS

The grown-ups told him that he was bundled by angels
and brought forth kicking and screaming in a hammock
pulled by a stork; then when he asked why in the pasture
the bull kept trying to ride the humped back of the heifer,
their nursery rhyme answer seemed wise—
why not bulls, if over the moon a cow jumps high?
He trusted them, his parents, with the bees and the birds;
everything they said untied the hard knots of riddles—
he blamed the sandman for bedroom moans and sighs.
He knew the cloth on his back kept his nakedness packed,
and behind zippers his unmentionable was hidden.
About girls, their spices and confections were tested and true.
Of course he would never peek under doors or dresses.
Goodness was keeping his short trousers from slipping,
and there were things best left to the bundlers in heaven.

THE STORYTELLER'S GOD

Yes once
I had an uncle
who told stories.
And in the middle
of every tale
he ever told me
a sort of god
would rise up from
nowhere. Years now
I've kept his truth
as mine—same god
when I'm talking
to myself. Even
people I've never
met before, they
tell me how a
sort of god is
there. And right in
the middle of stories
I've never heard
before, he comes.
Just as my uncle
told me. As I
have told myself
for years.

THE ACHE TO STAY ALIVE

He came to love his first love when she hurt him,
and he left her when the pain was slight—
he kept probing his happy heartache
and smiling cuts. With each beautiful infection
he felt at ease with the sore world.

His next love was so perfect he betrayed her;
he laughed until he cried. And she?
She wanted him until she died.
Such dog-eat-dog affairs were sweet—
they taught him tenderness.

Like most men, he wanted wealth,
a season's ticket to the ballpark,
fame, and raw meat. They gave him the swing shift
and the same routine. When he stopped caring
the world rushed back to kiss his feet.

When people near to him gave up and died,
he found it difficult to hide his thoughts.
He rocked his sighs to death and lied with tears.
Such mourning made him more alive.
The obituaries get read before the comics.

It has been this way since he can remember—
a continual mixing of pain and pleasure.
He has become an expert in such matters.
He has much knowledge of his thrashed life.
He is sick of the world, but he wants to stay.

CONFESSIONS OF AN AGING RUNNER

Because I am her father's age
not someone she expects to see
out running in shorts on a hot day
her laughter causes me to run faster
I tighten the slack flesh at my belt
brush back the wet strings of my hair
square my shoulders to smash the air
and I can feel the marbles of her eyes
rolling up and down my thick thighs—
she can never see me as I am
she can only think of me as someone
out of place in a fool's race
someone who should be resting in the shade
not angrily outrunning old age
she doesn't know I am overtaking myself
as I gulp the raw air and rush
like an aging bull stampeding.

WARM BREAD

So often I think
of a woman who
is many years dead.

I was too young
and selfish once
to know or share
her grief.

       Now I
miss her beautiful hands
and speak only
as a son can speak
and think of the things
we left unsaid.

       All this
whenever I break
into a piece of
warm bread.

THAWING OUT AFTER NEW ENGLAND

I had to get away
from my family and take
a European-Jewish wife and live
in five different countries before I found
my heart was packed
in New England ice. Because I was
brought up to dread pleasure and told
that sex was dirt, the evolution
of my love life had been slow.
I didn't become accomplished overnight.
My Semitic woman had to loosen
up her Anglo-Saxon puritanical slug
of lead by coaxing him to make love
in a lighted bedroom on a coverless bed.
Such frivolities would not occur
in a small and sexless New England town.
I'm thankful my wife wasn't born
in that land of ice people call
"beautiful New England." What would
the two of us do late at night?
I ask this because not once in my life
did I see my father kiss my mother.
They lived like straight winter oaks
swaying and crackling their branches of snow.
My only regret now is that I became
hot-blooded late in life. Lovemaking
where I come from is
walking on thin ice,
and after it's all over you drown.

II A PATCHWORK OF POEMS

NIGHT FOG

All night the fog
runs uphill
to haunt the sure-
footed trees. The open
mouth of the valley
has an evergreen
breath, and the heart-
beat of the marsh
is bobolink steady.
The brook delivers
its long oration
as it stumbles
clumsily downhill.
Above the trees
a stampede of clouds—
stallions harnessed
with rain. Too soon
the drawn face of
daylight reappears.
There will be no more
galloping horses
when night is gone
and the fog clears.

TOMBOUCTOU

Same street   same faces   you get tired   you want
to leave   people know you well

You take the book down   the one you placed out
of   reach   the one you say you'll never touch   never
take to turn the pages over

It's there   still there   the colored maps   the names
and then you wonder   where?   where shall I go?

Your thumb touches a river   suddenly you see   it's
something you never knew   something in you   where are
you going?

Now it's there   under your thumb   beside a river
somewhere in Africa   Burma   Greece

Some part of you that's never lived   something you
need to find   that somewhere that comes after why?
where must you go?

THE PRIVATE LIVES OF THE TOOLS

This is the land of measurements and cuts;
the world of cross-threaded nuts and sheared bolts.
It's here the awl still keeps its rapier poised,
and the adjustable wrenches, true to their multipurposes,
still have the saliva of grease about their mouths.
The snarled wig of a paintbrush soaks
in a shampoo of turpentine, and the tiptoeing nails
wait for the heavy tread of a hammer.
A bubble breaks on the watery breath of a level
as the pliers swoop like eagles on the tool rack,
and the dentures of the handsaws gleam with oil.
It's here the drills tunnel into planks and metal,
and the chisels lick shavings from the wood.
Up and down the boards and into the hard muscles
of steel these tools become sly and alert
as they travel through sawdust, grease and dirt.

TELEPHONE POLE

You're all
spine. Up
and down
a strand
of stiff
hair your
voice slides.
Your breath
is warm
and cold
air. In
a high
wind you
sigh. You've
got no
eyes. Clouds
give you
tears. Time
turns you
gray. On
one leg
you stand
for years.

SANTA IN THE MALL

He bounces all the Alices on his Wonderland lap
as he slowly shakes his dunce's cap and whispers
chimney talk and lies about his plastic team
of reindeer. His laughter comes too quickly as he wipes
the sore of a smile from his bandaged face
and lowers his eyes to a long list of promises
he won't keep. His fat-man cheer
grows louder as he drags his empty sack
across the twinkling meadows of the mall.
Then he shakes his bent bells at all who come
to hear his archaic tales about an arctic workshop
and the dexterity of elves. Someone should give him
a new suit of clothes and barber his chin
to remind him of all the perils and woes
of twentieth-century man. His midnight sleigh
is a merchant's chariot, and his chimney stops
behind the high-stepping Dancer, Prancer, etc.
are a jet lag joke. He looks like someone
who would be emptying a stocking, not filling it full.

THE MITCHELLS

They don't
care if
a cloud
scrapes its
back on
the sky
or a
tree wrings
its cut
hands. They
know that
fall is
here. It's
time for
them to
bank the
house, saw
and stack
the wood,
put on
their bright
bright coats
and kill
the deer.

SWEAT

I tell you sweat is
a sacrament I've
never understood.
It's just as familiar
as bread—I've
seldom had one
without the other.
                              Sweat
is an unexplored creek:
I was cutting brush
by a brook that led
nowhere. Just
under my shirt
I felt the trickle
of a galley slave's blood—
a bleeding older
than understanding.
                              Sweat
can move me gently.
It's an ox's tongue
nudging the lick.
A dumb caressing.
A baptism
of the hayfield,
the stone quarry,
the slit trench.

THE SKY

I tell you the sky is
big-bellied and gets
its way. Nobody pushes
the clouds around or yells
back when it thunders. It
is a bully. Whenever it gets
black, you will begin
to wonder aloud: who
is going to get caught;
get struck? The sky is
insane. And I tell you
we are, to keep looking up;
yes trying to forget
it is hungry; we know someone
is going to get hurt.

FART

There is a comical little methane ghost
hiding in your pants. He is a brash
stuntman or a talented vaudevillian—
maybe a frustrated aviator who wants to fly.
There are so many things this little loudmouth could be.
But loved and admired, he is never.
When people hear him sing they turn away,
and the lonesome lyrics of his sad song
end in a pitiful whine. The coarse bouquet
of his breath, blooming heavy as lilacs,
soon fades, though the memory of his presence
lingers in the minds of dinner guests.
He will often provoke laughter in a quip,
and when you think of him underwater
or blatantly screaming to be recognized
among strangers, you can only shake your head.
He is the Cicero of your stomach when you have dined
on oysters and canapes or gulped your turnip and cheese.
You may not like the way he haunts
your toilet bowl or struts across your underwear
with muddy feet, but when he is ready to recite
his baked bean psalms or pontificate on your nutrition
you owe it to yourself to hear him out.

SKIN

You do hold us in
with your blemishes and freckles
and the funny way you
zipper our scrapes and cuts.
Even your method of draping
blue-black curtains over our bruises
catches amazement. So you weren't made
to smooth old scars and wrinkles.
By aches and itches we decorate you
with salves and scratches. Belly-deep
in weight or close to the bone
you follow us all on this ride.
Up and down the slopes of our bodies,
under our armpits, between out toes,
we want your rind to surround us
with a suede tough enough to live in.

WORLD OF THE WASTED YEARS

He rises from a bed
of twisted pillows and sheets—his tongue
a burr from the all-night beer, his clothes
a scarecrow upon a chair.

                                    Shirt wrinkled
like a pharaoh's chest, belt curled
like an adder, hair thicker than
a hawk's nest—he stumbles down the stairs.

A full bowl of sunlight,
a rim of clover, and new tears
of dew on his crying pant cuffs—
over the hill to the mouth of the beach
he goes.

                        The world is stretching
grotesquely; stretching in circles of gold.
Eighteen years are behind him.
He tells himself he will never be old.

TAKING CHANCES

I skidded into
the ditch. I spun
backwards until the frame
of my pickup caught
on the frozen lip of a culvert—
ten miles from town. Ahead,
a faded lopsided sign
read: Road Discontinued.
Sleet hived the windshield
as I stepped down—bareheaded,
without an overcoat.
My shoes sponged the ground,
no jack, no log to pry loose
the truck. Sleet turned
to snow—no place to go,
nothing to do. The gas
ran out as the snow
began to drift. It was
nearly dark when a skidder
stopped in the pines.
Someone I knew. My voice
rode on the wind's back.
The woodsman waved
when my headlights flashed.
He gave me coffee and siphoned
gas from the skidder's tank
and pried loose the pickup
with a rock maple pole.
I slued into the drifts
and out. Got turned

34

around. Thanked him
and drove back to town.
Came home late. Sat down
and wrote this poem
about taking chances.

WELL WATER

Whenever I push
a stone cover
from a deep well,
I tell myself
it's far better
to believe in my
own magic; far
more appealing
to say to oneself:
right down where
the stars can be seen
from a deep well,
one should find
the coldest and best
tasting water.

ONE STAYS WHERE HE IS

One stays where he is—only the landscape moves.
One learns of the intricate self by rushing into the trap:
the being aware that going somewhere never happens.
There is always the same place one comes to after the trip;
always the excitement of mapping oneself on a map.

HARD CIDER

On winter nights
the lonesome time
would come, and we
would dream of summer
and the hot sun.
Then the glitter
of hard cider—
in the lamplight
our faces would shine.
The tall pitcher
would tinkle as
we poured its glow,
and each tumbler
would listen as
we emptied our hearts

THE WAITING

She is waiting for her mate
to reappear. The one
with white thighs and horns
cracked? Perhaps that one
or the lame Durham
of two years back. Beside
the worn gate she waits.
Her legs are spread wide.
She looks at the bars. She wants
to jump from the green lap
of grass onto the path
that circles the barn.

39

STAR COUNT

I went out to count the stars
believing the same number
would count the things I had.

But there were stars and more stars
and the needlework of the night
was stitched so delicately

a pinprick in the sky
would have injured the Great Bear;
would have emptied the Big Dipper.

ROBIN

A baby
robin fell
from its nest.
We fed it swabs
of hamburg and egg
on a matchstick.
We watched it fly
from one hand to
the next. The baby
feathered and grew
fat. It soon
perched in our hair
and fluttered at
the windows like
a rag. One day
we took the bird
into the woods
and placed it on
a limb. A sigh
of relief sobbed
in our throats as
the robin flew out
of our lives. An
experience like this
convinces us
that life is good.

FOR WHEN YOU GO

Take the apples when you go
and take the boughs and the early shadows
that slide westward and the jeweled stain
that blazes all morning in the grass
after a night of rain.

Take the road that circles the pines—
it furrows the hill and crosses the river.
Take the sunlight on the trees
and the voices of the waterfall
and the whispers as you sink to your knees
in moss around the pool.

Take the birches, the stillness, the path
up the mountain, the uncertain doe
licking her fawn, take the twilight,
and the moments after a thrush's call.
Take them when you go.

III   TRANSLATIONS   FROM   THE   LOWLANDS

IMAGINE

(From the Dutch of Remco Campert)

Imagine: we were snowbound
The food was almost gone
The radio broken, shoes leaked
Notebooks full of memories
We burned for a scanty warmth.

And the flag we had somewhere
Hidden we used as
A blanket of course. There was
Absolutely no hope
Not even hope for hope. Still

I was not unhappy because
Death was coupled with
So many statements of love
From you to me, me to you
That I could not

Achieve unhappiness. Time
Was lacking. There were always
Breasts to kiss, eyes
To reveal, and when we were tired
We slept and dreamt of

President Roosevelt.

DRAWING BOOK

(From the Dutch of Maurits Mok)

Daily there are wonders. My father comes
every evening out of the world space
into the warm house, clears his throat
and lets loose his worries. My mother covers
them with a handful of words. That starts
the human in me to move:
faces become stars, arms reach
from above to below through the cool
blue of another night, every word has
a resonance that makes me shiver.
And later, when I plunge to my sleep,
at the end of my thoughts, I see again
the drawing book of a hidden hand.

MORNING ON THE YSSEL

(From the Dutch of Nico J. Wilkeshuis)

maybe this mist is
the key to the secret of time and space
unfortunately the philosophers are still asleep
they dream of love or dream of traveling
this moment there is no one in the world
but a fisherman standing on the bank
now and then he pulls up a small cloud of mist
a brave little ship
distant and invisible
is puffing through the gray universe
the church bell: six blows of cotton wool
they fall like pillows on the world

now the whistling window cleaner is coming
to wipe the blurred windows
of the new day

IN THE PARK

(From the Dutch of K. Schippers)

Not the policeman with the bicycle
who stands near the blue teahouse
not the man by the river
what he sees I can't tell
not the woman with the baby carriage
who is coming in my direction
it's the old man on the bench
and I on the other bench
we both see
see how my carpet of bread crumbs
becomes a carpet of sparrows

THE SCHOOL SATCHEL SEEN AT CLOSE QUARTERS

(From the Dutch of Ellen Warmond)

Three dry elderly Englishmen
all descendants from a branch of Leicester
climb in mountain shoes to the hotel terrace
as if they wished to mount a parasol
seat themselves carefully in their creased skins
(But fairy tales stand cooling on the tea tray
even mermaids swim here with snorkels)

and behind them the widow
from Göttingen admires the panorama
that enlarges her view of the handsome
sunburned Spanish pimp in the bathing trunks
envelops him in a fat German daydream
full of sehnsucht leidenschaft and whipped cream

and already in all the Spanish churches
the people begin to pray for their salvation
an aging corpulent Lorelei
makes the whalebones of her swimsuit sing

TWO POEMS

(From the Dutch of P.M. Croiset)

I PLAY KING OEDIPUS

tenderness my mother never showed me
I cannot remember a kiss
but before she died she said
she loved me
because I looked like my father

INSTINCT

the seagulls stand
with their faces to the storm

I can imagine them turned around

I'm surprised
I still have arms
and legs

AIR CASTLE

(From the Flemish of Paul Snoek)

I wish, before I change
into a rock, an ant
or a poppy,
to become the creator
of an air castle.

I shall cut the roof
out of wrapping paper,
fold the rooms
from damp newspapers
and on the walls of sheet music
I shall paint laughing faces
behind windows
with metal ink.
In my castle shall live
doves of old silver.

I shall, before I change
into a stone, an animal
or a creeping plant,
become the creator
of an air castle,
for I have
the soft hands
of an inventor.

BALLAD OF A GENERAL

(From the Flemish of Paul Snoek)

Red from glory and fat from defeats
washing himself with steaming water
the general stands in front of the window
of his only room.

The women of his career
cut at two sides,
for his stomach is hairy
with the kisses of swords.

Despondently the general lets
his manly breasts, acquired
during a campaign in Europe,
hang resignedly.

Wet from water and red from Waterloo,
the general stands in front of
the only window of his room
drying himself with the tricolor.

SPANISH CAPRICCIO

(From the Flemish of Jos Vandeloo)

I forgot your name
was it Anita
or Carmen
or just simply Maria?

there are so many stars
planets
and women

there are so many Anitas
Carmens
and Marias

many atoms
form one body
many women
form many memories

was your name Anita
or Carmen
or just simply Maria?
I forgot your name
but not your body.

SELDOM DOES ONE SUCCEED

(From the Dutch of Guillaume van der Graft)

Seldom does one succeed in
                    writing
in such a simple way
that each word is a child
breathing in the
bed of the language
under the blanket of the poem.
Writing in such a way isn't
                    easy.
Sometimes one wakes up
the small child
who asks for something
                    impossible.
Give him something; anything
you don't understand.
Then turn on the lights,
and sit for a long time on the
edge of the language reading
what he says
word for word
hand in hand.

POEM

(From the Flemish of Adriaan de Roover)

long long after the wind
fled from the hides of animals
fled from the fish-scale leaves
the trees were still dizzy
I am cold in the forest
now I want to wash my words
with evening moss and dark water
my words have become dirty
living in the mouths of thousands

.

DUALITY

(From the Dutch of Andries Poppe)

I stand with my heart in one hand
and my head in the other hand,
and to the rhythm of the wind I sway
back and forth between dream and intellect.
No matter how much I try,
I never remain balanced:
seen from the left, I'm a number;
considered from the right, I'm a poem.
My skull is full of perceptions
that my inclinations can't touch;
and what my heart tells my lips
my head has never understood.

HERON

(From the Dutch of Hans Warren)

Small silent bird
bowed at the water's edge
the winter bounces gray from your eyes
ebb and flood push whispering
through endless creeks
a brittle reed breaks
bird that half listens
to the tossing of a distant fish
and half frozen with lack
buries his beak in his feathers

EVENING

(From the Dutch of Ellen Warmond)

Seconds walk angrily backwards
the day has toppled out of time

I become as silent as a beach
on a winter's night   I become
as empty as a fire-gutted
house   life stands further
away from me than I can tell

lay your face in your hands
and try to imagine this

METAMORPHOSIS

(From the Dutch of Ellen Warmond)

We knew
that time mercilessly consumes
like a whole army
of hungry caterpillars

but not
that it would suddenly reveal itself
to this moment
full of marvelous butterflies

RODRIGUEZ

(From the Dutch of Mea Strand)

He is back
rodriguez
red and shaggy
with bare feet
quickly each cobblestone
kisses a toe
see there steps
rodriguez
big black see
the oiled knee
the loose sweater
embraces his neck
a black left eye
passes above me
like a painted man
on a vase
rodriguez
rodriguez is loose

ON THE HELMETS

(From the Dutch of Nico Verhoeven)

On the helmets of thunderheads
there romps an amorous spring sun.
The city builds itself in bird flight.
The café terraces become and El Dorado again
with their parasols and light activity.
The whole day is an album of photos;
in the evening one turns the pages and sighs.
In the evening one thinks of the coming day,
of the evening with the embezzled light,
of the evening itself; a fence of worries
twilights the book. One closes it.

ARIA OF THE GROWNUP

(From the Dutch of Alfred Kossmann)

When she comes home too late
Smelling of air and street
I search in my strict reception
Between care and punishment
The sublime balance
And we dance on points of rope
I anger, she repentance
I hardness, she asking for help
I forgiveness, she thankfulness
Till we in subtle glow
Blue of eye, red of cheek
Make up, bow and leave
Last stance in the pas dedeux
Last glance in the warm dance
Which she will later, more lightly
Lovingly dance with her dolls
And who with me?

VANISHING POEM

(From the Dutch of J. Bernlef)

Where do I find the word
that hasn't died in a poem?
I shall look for it as a
child looks for a self-made kite
that trembles and falls and rises;
a kite that slowly lifts in the sky
and at last vanishes.

SNOW

(From the Flemish of Gaston Burssens)

Sparrows chirp loudly
cars hum louder
trams ring loudest

Through the centuries stars are
symbols of ideal desire
snowballs star open
snow is white on black
camouflage

when the king is in Nice
the court jester throws snowballs
the footmen ride in sleighs
with the members of the parliament

The sparrows fly forlornly
and chirp loudly
the barometer points to changeable
snow is camouflage
on Christmas night no baby will be born
in a garage

FUGUE FOR LIDY

(From the Dutch of Han Foppe)

this is a time of weeping willows
I said
you nodded and sighed yes
this is the time when the clouds
lean over towards the unknown
a time of empty hands
this is a time of weeping willows
I said
and you were crying

LULLABY

(From the Dutch of Nico J. Wilkeshuis)

between us
stands a piano
the tones are paper boats
cryboats blue
laughboats yellow
and boats of desire
that take you through the mist
then they blow
as fragments through the rainy world
where the moon is sad
and lights blink in a wet street
go to sleep
and count the boats in your dream

IV FABLES AND HANG-UPS

GREAT AMERICAN SUCCESS STORY

When the young girl ran off
with the salesman from the city
he promised her broadway & clothes
& she left behind her
an angry old pa who willed
all his money to the d. a. r. &
shortly afterwards the girl
came back without the salesman
& she being lonely & big
in the belly couldn't say no
when certain overtures were made
by the scrawny & pimply boy
who worked downtown as a soda jerk.
This particular story took place
a long time ago. The girl
is now a fat matron & her husband
owns the drugstore & her episode
with the salesman was a youthful
indiscretion better forgotten than
dwelt upon. When her only offspring
asks about grandpa's money,
she tells him there never was any.
There was only the drugstore,
hard times & the great american
success story as lived & boldly
breathed by the step-pa & the off-
spring has heard all this before.

MR. FOUR LETTERS

Mr. Four Letters asked a pretty girl to visit him. One evening she knocked at his door. Mr. Four Letters was in his dining room eating one of his meager dinners. He muttered to himself when he heard the knocking. He lived alone, and he enjoyed having his small nourishment without interruptions, but he did get up and go to the door to see who was there. He was very surprised to see the girl, and he was delighted that she had come to his house. He never really thought she would be in his section of town.

"Come in, come in," Mr. Four Letters chanted.

The girl entered. She looked around until she found his bedroom and immediately took off her clothes and sat on his bed.

This surprised Mr. Four Letters much more than seeing the girl at his door.

"Why do you take off your clothes?" he asked with bewilderment.

"I need you," she replied.

"But why take off your clothes, my child?" he asked again.

"You are Mr. Four Letters, aren't you?"

"Yes, of course."

"You did ask me to visit you," the girl reminded him.

Before Mr. Four Letters could stop her, she was rubbing herself on his white bedspread.

"I'm the elderly Mr. Four Letters," the old gentleman explained.

The girl was puzzled.

"Then why did you ask me here?"

"To help you," he answered.

"To help me!" she said astonished. "Where is your son?"

"Kiss?" he said with irritation.

"I really wanted to see the other one," the girl replied, sitting up.

"My grandson and I are not on speaking terms," Mr. Four Letters said with much dignity.

"Then what is your name?" the girl asked as she stared at him.

"Love," the old gentleman said.

The pretty girl fell back on Love Four Letter's white bedspread and laughed until she wept.

MALTESE GIRL

She is beautiful when she stands
with the trinket of her hand pinned
to the side of her raised skirt.

Is it any wonder that the people
who love her are shocked and hurt?
Six months after she has wed

her body thickens. Not yet pregnant,
she waddles from her marriage bed
like a sow to the front steps.

She hooks a string of sausages
around the handle of a pail, squats
like a mountain that has lost its lava,

and with the bubble of an arm behind
a brush, she scours her husband's footprints
from the stoop without looking up.

MR. REPEAT

Mr. Repeat is a bank clerk who loves his work. Every morning he would enter the vault and wheel a big metal cart to his cage. He would take the money from the cart and stack the bills and coins in huge piles around him. At nine o'clock the door of the bank would be unlocked and the people would rush to his cage to have him count their bills and coins. Mr. Repeat would count a stack of bills and coins and he would look at the clock over the bank door. Then he would count again.

Mr. Repeat always went home at five o'clock to eat his dinner and to talk about the bank with his wife. On Sundays Mr. Repeat would think about the bank; he would think about the coins and the bills. When he got tired of this, he would think about the clock over the bank door and the people who came into the bank. On Monday morning Mr. Repeat was always the first employee to enter the vault. Mr. Repeat is a bank clerk who loves his work.

One day Mr. Repeat counted a stack of bills and looked at the clock. He saw a man in a green coat who was coming into the bank. Mr. Repeat counted another stack of bills and looked at the clock. He saw another man in a green coat who was coming into the bank.

That night Mr. Repeat talked and talked about the two men in green coats who had come into the bank. When his wife asked him what time of day it had been, he couldn't tell her. He couldn't even remember the men clearly.

The next morning Mr. Repeat was the last employee to enter the vault. His fellow employees looked at him curiously, but they said nothing.

That afternoon Mr. Repeat counted a stack of bills and looked at the clock. He saw a man in a green coat at the door of the bank. Mr. Repeat counted a stack of bills and looked at the clock. He saw a man in a green coat at the door of the bank. Mr. Repeat counted a stack of bills and looked at the clock....Mrs. Repeat is still cooking dinner. It's always four o'clock in the afternoon. The bank never closes.

Mr. Repeat is a bank clerk who loves his work.

THE TULLIVER BOY

Daily, there is
that weathercock turn of his head
to see if someone sneaks
behind him. Then the sore
of a smile on his stiff face,
and people say: "There goes
the Tulliver boy running
loose in the streets." No one
knows he's chained and the town
is staggering out of sight;
no one knows he's hearing
a Sousa march. Who would
guess there is a cadence
as he chants around a corner?
"I've got a c-r-a-z-y father.
a c-r-a-z-y mother!" And then
he gargles his laughter; prances
up the street. He's happy to be
his own beast.

HOUSE OF HANG-UPS

If you peel off the skin
and shove aside the crisscross
of muscles around this back
and chest, a small child
will approach you—head
down but arms out-
stretched.

       And he will take
your hand and lead you back
to where his world began:
to a woman too much in love
with a spoiled-brat man,
to a house that swallows you whole,
to a tableful of in-laws
in a bellyache of rooms.

       The child
will show you the intricate mechanism
of a wrinkle and how it works
like a time bomb on a smile
or how the shrug of a shoulder
can be deadlier than a slapped
face or how the arch
of a drooping eyebrow annihilates.

And the child will lead you
to the bedsprings that chatter

in vacant rooms, to the club-
footed print of a flat-
iron in the foxglove wallpaper,
to the torn mattress
and the kicked Christmas tree.

             There is
even a place to hide when words
become coarse and ugly.
But coaxing won't get the child
to show you this. He drops
your hand and runs off to
be there alone.

             When the child
comes back, he won't even
touch you. What he wants now
is a scarf of muscles wrapped
around him and a tight
bandage of skin.

HOUSE GUESTS

It all begins
when I shake hands
and say to them
how long it's been!
Since I insist
they'll spend the night.
Next day I wait
for them to leave
but they don't go
and I pretend
how good it is
and so much fun.
Then all week long
they talk and eat.
There is so much
to do and say
I can't break in.
From pantry to
bedroom is how
a long day ends.
Finally, I
ask them to leave
but they don't hear.
I try to drag

them from the house
and all I get
is a handful
of air. When I
go outside they
lock themselves in.
They don't look up
when I rap at
windows; they don't
even come to
the door. This is
my place, I keep
shouting at them—
my house! But I'm
beginning to
think I don't live
here anymore.

THE CUCKOO MAN

(A Fable)

A long time back
they told about
an old guy who was
crazy and didn't care
a damn about money
and time. And one day
when he was fed up
with the precise world, he got out
his jackknife and carved
a cuckoo from a block of wood.
The carving felt dead
in Sigmund Friedrich
Hexenfresser's hands,
and being a cynical old man,
he stuck a taut spring
in the cuckoo's arse.
This gimmick led to a sprocket,
a chain, and a homemade
squawk box that said
cuckoo
cuckoo
cuckoo
whenever the mechanism was set off.
People who knew the old man

said he was mad. And his wife—
a bulging *Frau* who worshipped
the practicalities of life—said
"Sigmund Friedrich Hexenfresser,
do something sensible!
Don't be a fool!"   So then Sigmund—
to taunt his wife, his friends,
and the world—wired
the cuckoo to a clock. Fun
at last, he thought.
cuckoo
cuckoo
cuckoo
            The whole world loved
Sigmund and his clock. The honorable
Herr Sigmund Friedrich Hexenfresser
became wealthy and fat. But he never
had peace after that. The old guy
should have known that people love
the damndest things, but most of all
the crazy inventions made
by crazy men.

MR. LAVENDER

Mr. Lavender's unpainted bungalow was located between Mr. Black's green bungalow and Mr. Brown's white bungalow on a five-house street. Across the road from Mr. Lavender's property, Mr. Green lived in his brown bungalow. Next to Mr. Green, Mr. White lived in his newly painted black bungalow. Mr. White was the only man on the five-house street who had a sense of humor.

The wives of the four humorless men and Mrs. White always met on Sunday to talk over such harmless things as budgeting and their husbands. The five male colors convened in one of the five kitchens to drink beer and to talk seriously about fishing and playing golf. Sometimes they talked about drinking while drinking.

One afternoon they consumed more beer than they usually did on a weekend, and their conversation took a strange turn. Mr. White playfully suggested that Mr. Lavender's bungalow should be painted. Mr. Lavender was feeling very happy, and he was only too eager to agree with Mr. White. But the color? They were all very bewildered when they tried to think of a color.

"Such a serious undertaking must be given much thought," the cautious Mr. Black told the other men.

"Agreed," said Mr. Green. Mr. Green was always very agreeable.

All week long the five men thought about the unpainted bungalow. The next Sunday they talked and talked about it. There seemed to be no solution. All

the following week their nights were sleepless as they
worried over the selection of a color.

"I guess it will have to remain colorless," Mr. Lavender
said wearily.

"Perhaps it's just as well," Mr. Brown said with a sigh.

"What do you mean by that?" Mr. Lavender snapped.

"What do you think I mean?" Mr. Brown snarled.
Mr. Brown was very irritated because of so much
thinking and so little sleep.

"Turn to stone," Mr. Lavender said crossly to Mr.
Brown.

"Turn to stone yourself," Mr. Brown replied.

"You all act like a pack of dogs," Mr. Black spoke up.

"Perhaps you should change your name, Lavender,"
laughed Mr. White.

But Mr. Lavender was aroused, and he told Mr. White
to turn to stone too.

The next Sunday the wives didn't meet and the men
didn't drink together. The street looked smaller. The
paint on the four painted bungalows definitely seemed
brighter in the sunshine.

One Sunday Mr. Lavender painted his bungalow black,
and shortly afterwards Mr. Black moved away. Then
Mr. Lavender repainted his bungalow green. Mr. Green
accepted a new but less lucrative position with his firm
in another city. Mr. Lavender was so pleased with
himself that he painted his bungalow a rich brown the
very next Sunday. Mr. Brown died Monday afternoon.

Mr. Lavender wasn't Mr. Lavender anymore. He
repainted his brown bungalow white. Mr. White
repainted his black bungalow lavender. White still had a
sense of humor. But Mrs. White was witty instead. She
left Mr. White. The poor man laughingly burned his
house one night. There wasn't anything else he could

do. He was still laughing when men in white jackets carried him away.

Mr. and Mrs. Lavender now are the only people who live on that small four-house street. Nobody wants to live in the empty buildings. Some people say that these three bungalows smell strongly of paint.

For years, Mr. Lavender has been painting his bungalow a new color every Sunday. He likes his work. Mr. Lavender is a house painter by trade.

THE EGOTIST'S HERE AND NOW

I remember saying to myself when standing
in a field under the noonday sun or walking
the streets of an unknown town or sitting
by a gray window at dusk: part of me
will never change; the here and now is mine
to see; this moment is caught like a cloverleaf
in a well-thumbed book.

                    Then I hear myself saying
to people I meet at jetports or on freeways
in the middle of the continent or in an elevator
stalled between floors: I have shared a moment
we both will remember; when we look back
to the here and now we will think of each other;
all this we will recall.

                    And I keep thinking—
more as reminder and less as conviction—when choking
on bread crumbs or bracing myself as the dentist drills
or letting my fingers worry an imaginary bunch:
I have been given the moment;
let me be grateful for what it is;
the here and now is mine to keep.

                    So many times
I have found contradictions—when repeating

some meaningless cliché, lying hopelessly to myself
or appearing wise, trying to stuff the cracks
in my chipped cup of memory: the here and now
is all I have; live for the moment; there is
no future and no past.

                        Have I become myself
by watching others lose their chances;
have I hardened myself with forgetfulness
and good intentions and lies? I will
prepare myself for the moment—let it stalk me
like the stray dog it is, ready to cringe
as I turn to throw these stones of thought.

ABOUT THE AUTHOR

C. J. Stevens has contributed poems, stories, Dutch and Flemish translations, articles, and interviews to more than five hundred publications and sixty anthologies and textbooks. He is the author of *Beginnings* and *Circling at the Chain's Length* (poetry); the biography *Lawrence at Tregerthen* (D. H. Lawrence in Cornwall), *The Next Bend in the River* (history and gold mining in Maine), *One Day With a Goat Herd* (animal behavior), and *The Folks from Greeley's Mill* (fiction). He is a native of Maine.

Concordia College Library
Bronxville, NY   10708